KING JESUS IS HIS NAME

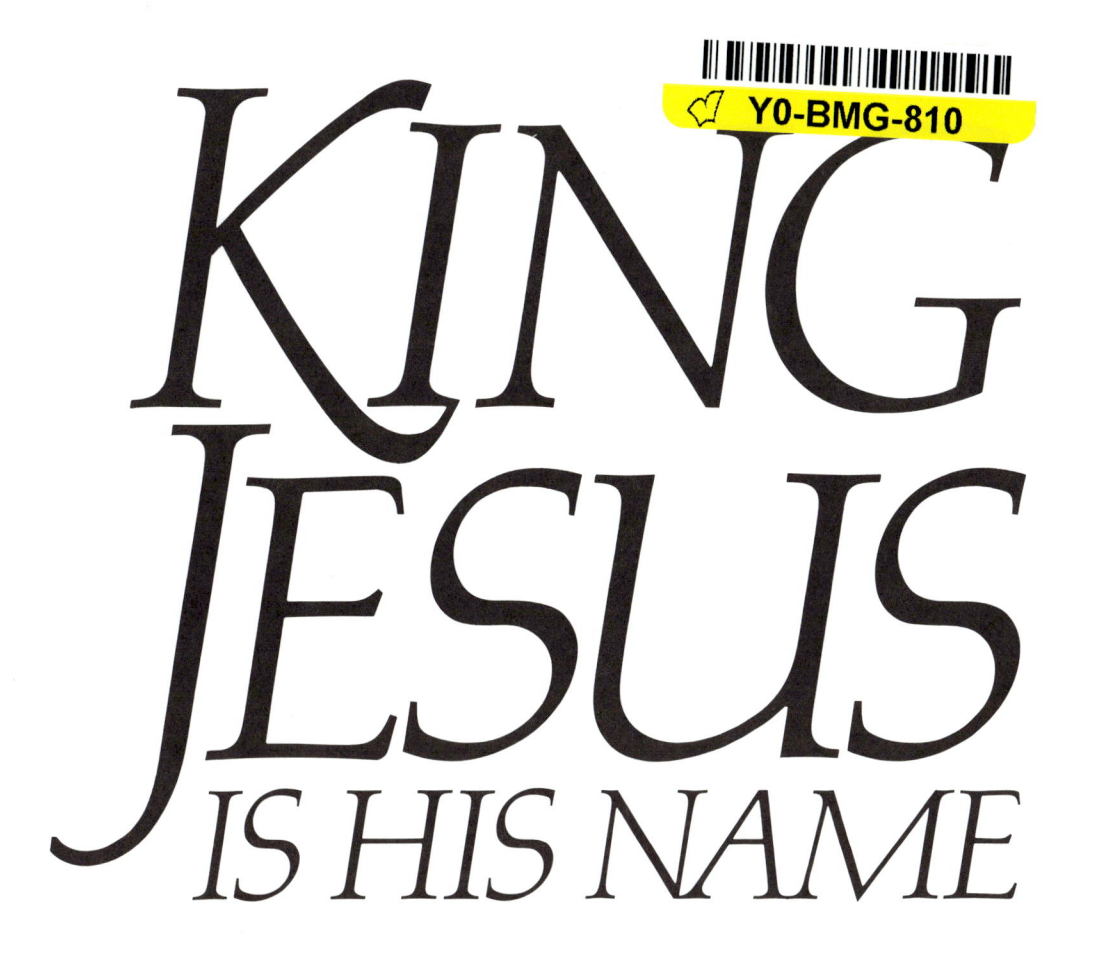

A Worship Musical for Christmas

ARRANGED BY
JOSEPH LINN

Lillenas PUBLISHING COMPANY

KANSAS CITY, MO 64141

Copyright © 1993 by Lillenas Publishing Co.
All rights reserved. Litho in U.S.A.

FOREWORD

Would you believe this year I put our Christmas lights on our house Thanksgiving weekend and waited until late January to take them down. I *love* the Christmas season! I like the carols, the decorations, the crisp winter air—and all the special events that encompass this time of year.

Several years ago, while recording another Christmas project, my engineer friend Don Enns asked, "Do we really need one more Christmas musical?" That was a fair question. The answer is NO if we are speaking about a new message. The wonderful news of Christ's coming to earth as the Savior-Redeemer is a message with which we should never tamper.

However, if the question is "Can we use new 'wrappings' and arrangements that hopefully put exciting, fresh Christmas music in the hands of church choirs?" the answer is definitely YES!

I pray that the musical *King Jesus Is His Name* will greatly enhance your Christmas musical celebration this year. May God bless you!

JOSEPH LINN
ARRANGER

King Jesus Is His Name is presented as an answer to the needs of churches looking for a mix of contemporary and traditional expressions of the season in a moderately easy musical format. Voicings are kept within a comfortable singing range, so the choir always sounds full and powerful, not forced or strained. Each arrangement works in its given SATB form, with optional cued notes for added color if desired.

Helpful notes on making this an outreach to your community are included (see pages 106-107). The real story of Christmas, so familiar to many of us who have heard it told and sung for years, can be a new experience for many others. We ask that you use this material in the spirit with which it was conceived and written: to be a means of reaching others with the joyful news that a King has come!

HARLAN MOORE
LILLENAS PUBLISHING COMPANY

At the request of the copyright owner, we include these lyrics to the first verse of "O Hearken Ye," which were not a part of "Manger Medley":
>O hearken ye who would believe,
>The gracious tidings now receive:
>Gloria, gloria in excelsis Deo.
>The mighty Lord of heav'n and earth,
>Today is come to human birth.
>Gloria, gloria in excelsis Deo.

Copyright © 1954 (renewed) and 1957 (renewed) Hollis Music, Inc., New York, N.Y. International copyright secured. Made in U.S.A. All rights reserved including Public Performance for Profit.

TABLE OF CONTENTS & PERFORMANCE PLANNER

SONG   **PAGE**   **REHEARSAL DATES**

I. HIS COMING—Jesus, the Promised One

- **Glory, Hallelujah Medley** 4   _____
  (When He Came; Glory, Hallelujah;
  Angels We Have Heard on High)
- **Angels Shouting,** with **Rejoice!** 14   _____
- Interlude I—The News of His Coming 22   _____
- **Manger Medley** 24   _____
  (Sweet Was the Song the Virgin Sang;
  No Room; Away in a Manger;
  O Hearken Ye)
- **King Jesus Is His Name** 38   _____

II. HIS MISSION—Jesus, the Savior

- **For Unto Us,** with **When He Came** 49   _____
- **Sweet Little Jesus Boy** 53   _____
- **Praise to the Savior Medley** 61   _____
  (We Have Come to Worship Thee;
  Beautiful Savior;
  Praise the Lord! Ye Heavens, Adore Him;
  Blessed Be the Name of the Lord;
  My Soul Magnifies the Lord)
- Interlude II—The Reason for His Coming 77   _____
- **Love Was When** 79   _____

III. HIS COMING AGAIN—Jesus, the Lord of All

- **When He Came** 88   _____
- **In Majesty He Will Come** 92   _____
- Interlude III—An Invitation 101   _____
- **Take Jesus with You** 103   _____

CHRISTMAS MUSICALS AS OUTREACH OPPORTUNITIES 106

FINAL REHEARSAL(S):

DATE _____ TIME _____

DATE _____ TIME _____

PERFORMANCE(S):

DATE _____ TIME _____ ARRIVE BY _____

DATE _____ TIME _____ ARRIVE BY _____

… 4

I. HIS COMING – JESUS, THE PROMISED ONE
Glory, Hallelujah Medley

Arr. by Joseph Linn

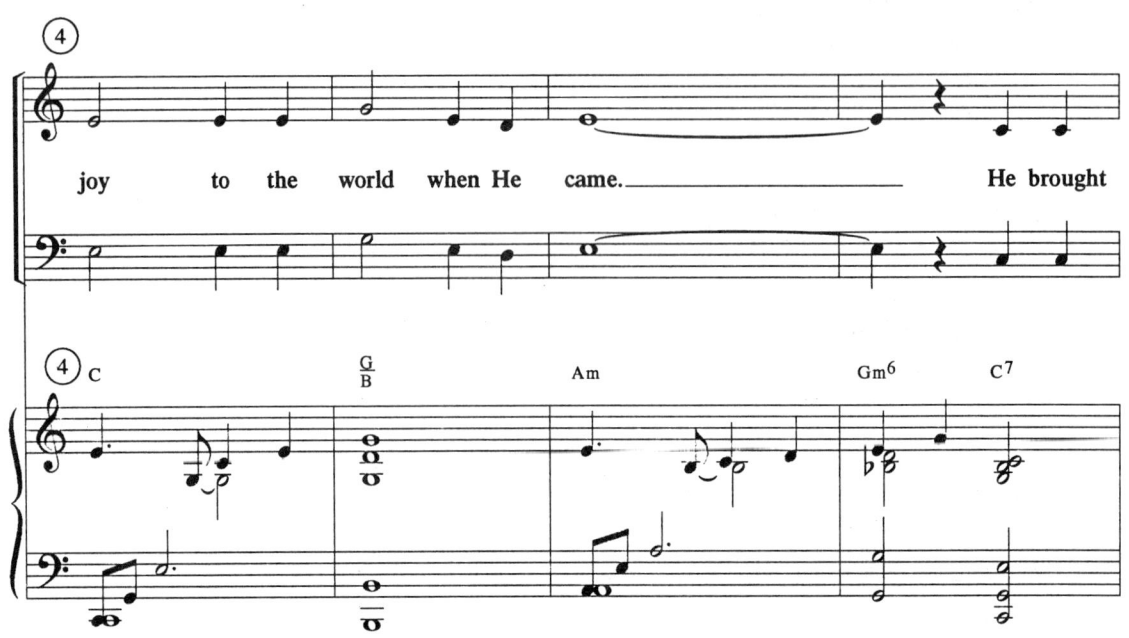

CD: 01 Gently, freely ♩ = ca. 72

*"When He Came" (Mosie Lister)

---

*Copyright © 1983, 1993 by Lillenas Publishing Co. All rights reserved.
Administered by Integrated Copyright Group, Inc., P.O. Box 24149, Nashville, TN 37202.

Arr. copyright © 1993 by Lillenas Publishing Co. All rights reserved.
Administered by Integrated Copyright Group, Inc., P.O. Box 24149, Nashville, TN 37202.

joy to the world when He came. To the

hearts heav-y-bur-dened with trou-bles and with strife, He brought

joy, great joy when He came, when He

came. He brought joy, great joy when He came.

31
*"Glory, Hallelujah" (Mark Kellner/Isaac Watts – Mark Kellner/G.F. Handel
mf Unison
1. Joy to the world, the Lord is come! Let earth receive her King.
2. Sing to the Lord a song of praise, For He has done great things.
Cadd9
Fadd9/C
G/C
35
No more let sins and sor - rows grow. Let heav - en and na - ture sing.
Un - to you is born this day A babe who is Christ the King.
Fadd9
G
Fadd9/G
Div.
f
39
Sing - ing glo - ry, hal - le -
C
F
G/F

lu - jah, Je - sus Christ has come!

Glo - ry, hal - le - lu - jah, Je - sus is God's own Son. Son.

He is the One that the proph-ets fore-told. Shep-herds and an-gels with won-der be-hold. All of the earth now with prais - es will ring, For Je - sus, the

CD: 05
ba - by, is born to be King, to be King.
Am/F♯
Dm/G
Gadd9
A♭sus
A♭add9
63
f
mel.
3. Joy to the world, the Lord is
tacet
come!
mel.
67
Let earth re - ceive her
Hal - le - lu - jah, glo - ry, glo - ry,
G♭
A♭

King. hal-le-lu-jah, a-men. Let ev-'ry heart pre-pare Him room, And heav-en and na-ture sing.

"Angels We Have Heard on High" (Trad. French Carol)

Glo-

12

13

Angels Shouting
with
Rejoice!

D. W.

DAN WHITTEMORE
Arr. by Joseph Linn

Driving ♩ = ca. 144

An - gels____ shout - ing,____ "Glo - ry to God___ in the high - est!"

Copyright © 1993 by Lillenas Publishing Co. All rights reserved.
Administered by Integrated Copyright Group, Inc., P.O. Box 24149, Nashville, TN 37202.

12
An - gels shout - ing, "Peace on earth, good will to men."
Unison mf Glo-ri-a,
12 Cadd9 C G/C Am/C F G C
16
An - gels shout - ing, "Glo-ry to God in the high - est!"
glo-ri-a Glo-ri-a,
16 Cadd9 C G/C C F/C C G/C C
20
CD: 08
Unison
An - gels shout - ing, "Peace on earth, good will to men." The
20 Cadd9 C G/C Am/C F G C

(24) Half-time feel

Lord has come from heav-en's glo-ry to live up-on this earth. O hear the an-gels tell the sto-ry pro-claim-ing the Mes-si-ah's birth.

cresc. Div. f

Glo - ry
Glo - ry to God, glo - ry to God in the high-

17

46 *"Rejoice!" (Linda Rebuck - David Huntsinger)

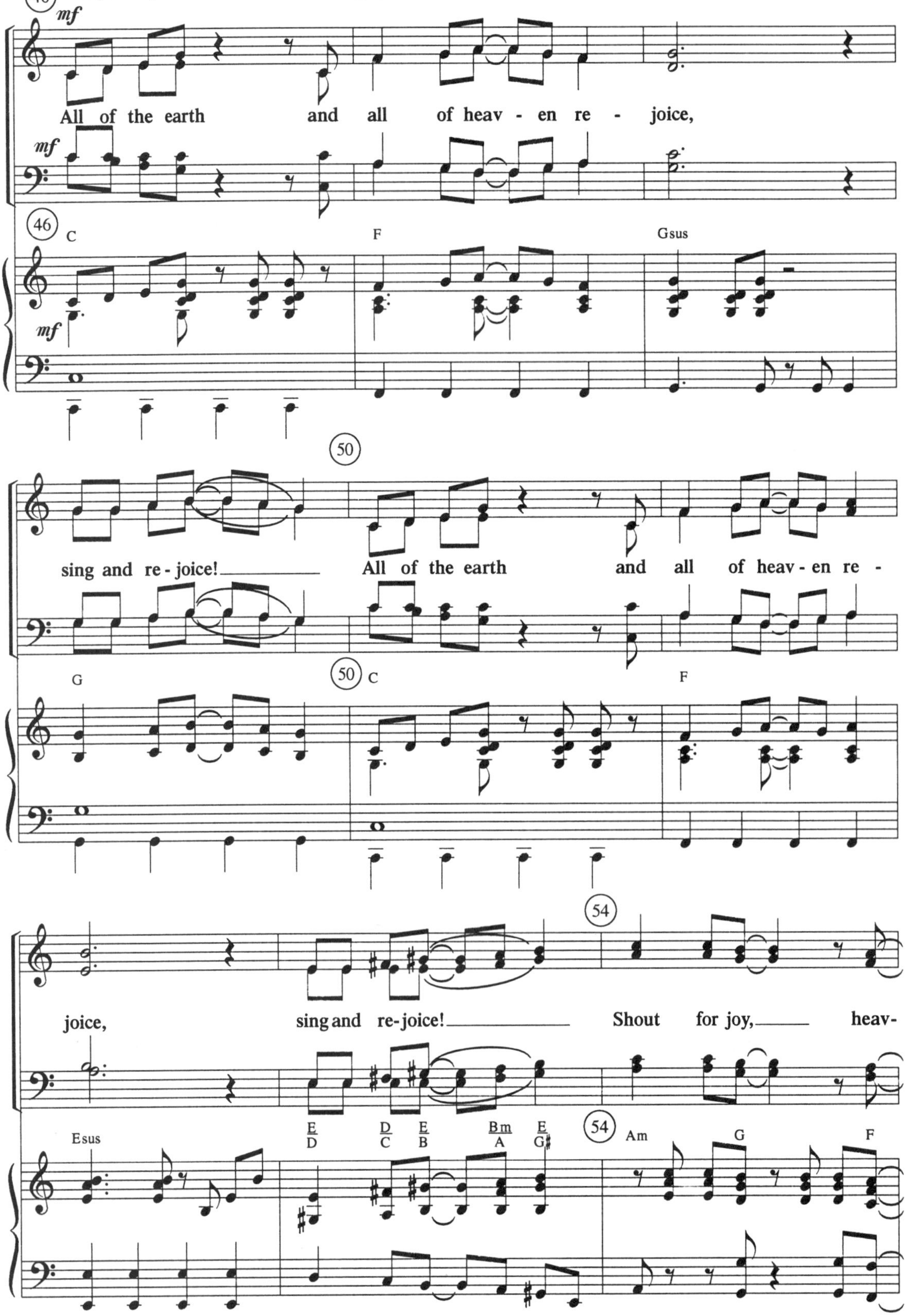

-en and earth. Cel - e - brate the Sav - ior's birth.

All of the earth and all of heav - en re - joice,

sing and re - joice!

64
mel. (a few sopranos should double the melody if needed)
All of the earth and all of heav - en re - joice,
Db
Gb
Absus
68
sing and re - joice!
All of the earth and all of heav - en re -
Ab
Db
Gb
mel.
72
joice,
sing and re - joice!
Shout for joy,
heav-
Fsus
F/Eb
Eb/Db
F/C
Csus/Bb
F/A
Bbm
Ab
Gb

21

Narr. 1 This was a celebration God had designed from the beginning, so He wanted to make sure the birth of His Son did not go by unnoticed. *(music begins)*

Interlude I – The News of His Coming

JOSEPH LINN

Across the centuries up to that very first Christmas night, God was whispering His plan to the world. To the prophet Isaiah, He said:

Narr. 2 "The virgin will be with child and will give birth to a son, and will call him Immanuel." *(Isa. 7:14, NIV)*

"For to us a child is born, to us a son is given, and the government will be on his shoulders. And he will be called Wonderful Counselor, Mighty God, Everlasting Father, Prince of Peace." *(Isa. 9:6, NIV)*

Narr. 1 To Micah He revealed the exact place Christ would be born:

Copyright © 1993 by Lillenas Publishing Co. All rights reserved.
Administered by Integrated Copyright Group, Inc., P.O. Box 24149, Nashville, TN 37202.

Narr. 2 "But you, Bethlehem . . . out of you will come for me one who will be ruler over Israel."
(Micah 5:2, NIV)

Narr. 1 To shepherds in the hills of Judea, God used an angelic army and celestial signs to proclaim:
Narr. 2 "Today in the town of David a Savior has been born to you; he is Christ the Lord."
(Luke 2:11, NIV)

Narr. 1 The birth of Jesus is possibly the most widely known single event in history. And because God placed such importance on it, we tell it to you once again. *(Interlude I ends)*

Narr. 2 The apostle Luke wrote these words: "In those days Caesar Augustus issued a decree that a census should be taken of the entire Roman world. So Joseph went up from the town of Nazareth to Bethlehem the town of David, because he belonged to the house and line of David. He went there to register with Mary, who was pledged to be married to him and was expecting a child. While they were there, the time came for the baby to be born, and she gave birth to her firstborn, a son. She wrapped him in cloths and placed him in a manger, because there was no room for them in the inn." *(Luke 2:1, 4-7, NIV)*

Manger Medley

Arr. by Joseph Linn

With emotion ♩ = ca. 136
CD: 12 tacet

"Sweet Was the Song the Virgin Sang" (William Ballet - *The Sacred Harp*)

2nd time: ladies unison

1. Sweet was the song the Virgin sang; To Beth-le-hem she came And
   Babe," sang she so ten-der-ly, With love, and joy, and mirth, In

2nd time: men unison (mel.)

Arr. © 1993 by Lillenas Publishing Co. All rights reserved.
Administered by Integrated Copyright Group, Inc., P.O. Box 24149, Nashville, TN 37202.

25

was de-liv-ered of a Son: Lo, Je-sus was His
awe and won-der gazed on Him, God's Son now come to

name. "Ah, lul-la-by, my joy!" Sing-ing,
earth. "Ah, He is born, God's Son!" Sing-ing,

2nd time: all, div.

"Lul-la-by, my Ba-by Boy." She
"He is born, God's ho-ly Son." In

was de-liv-ered of a Son: Lo, Je-sus was His name.
awe and won-der gazed on Him, God's Son now come to earth.

2. "Sweet

*"No Room" (John W. Peterson)
Solo
No room— on-ly a man-ger of hay. No room— He is a

D^{add9} G^6 Gm^6 D^{add9}

*Copyright © 1958, renewed 1986, arr. © 1993 by John W. Peterson Music. All rights reserved. Used by permission.

27

28

(40) No room— sure-ly the world is blind. No room.

(44) Choir
An - gels, in heav-en up yon - der, Watch with a-maze-ment and won - der To see the Son of the High-est treat-ed, treat-ed so!

poco rit.

29

"Away in a Manger" (Anon./J.T. McFarland - W.J. Kirkpatrick)

No room, no room, no room.
No room, no room.
No room, no room.

rit. ... accel.

Ladies unison

The cattle are lowing, the Baby awakes, But little Lord Jesus no

Gently

cry-ing He makes. I love Thee, Lord Jesus, look down from the sky And stay by my cradle till morn-ing is nigh.

Be near me, Lord Jesus, I ask Thee to stay Close by me for-ev-er, and love me, I pray. Bless all the dear children in Thy ten-der care, And

33

*"O Hearken Ye" (Wihla Hutson - Alfred Burt)

**O hearken ye who long for peace, Your troubled searching now may cease.

*Copyright © 1954 (renewed) and 1957 (renewed) Hollis Music, Inc., New York, NY. International copyright secured. Made in U.S.A. All rights reserved including public performance for profit.
**This arrangement uses the 2nd and 3rd stanzas of "O Hearken Ye". At the request of the copyright owner, the text for the first verse is included in the foreword.

Glo - ri - a, glo - ri - a, in ex - cel - sis De - o. For at His cra - dle you shall find God's heal - ing grace for all man - kind. Glo - ri - a, glo - ri - a, in ex - cel - sis De - o.

O heark - en ye who long for love, And turn your hearts to God a - bove.

Glo - ri - a, glo - ri - a, in ex - cel - sis De - o. The an - gel's song the won - der tells: Now Love In - car - nate with us dwells! Glo - ri - a,

glo - ri - a, in ex - cel - sis De -
C7/E C7 F Bb F/A Gm7 F/A Dm C7sus C C7
o. Glo - ri - a, glo - ri - a, in ex -
141
f
F Bb Gm/E F C7/E C7 F Bb F/A Gm
cel - sis De - o.
145
F/A Dm C7sus C C7 F

King Jesus Is His Name

B. M.

BABBIE MASON
Arr. by Joseph Linn

With energy ♩ = ca. 96

CD: 19

Born in a sta-ble late one night Un-der-neath a sky so star-ry bright. The star made the night shine like day, And the shep-herds came to bring Him praise. Wise-men bro't Him beau-ti-ful gifts,

Gold and myrrh and frank - in - cense. What did they call that lit-tle bit-ty ba - by?

Choir: King Je - sus is His name.

What did the heav-en-ly hosts pro-claim?

King Je-sus is His name.

Who would have tho't this ti-ny lad would hold all pow-er in His hand?

Oo

42

Tell me, what did they call Him?

King Je - sus is His

name.

The people came from all a-round, They knelt in awe of this King they found. The manger held such a ho-ly sight; This gift from heav'n would bring them life.

Life for-ev-er in a heav-en-ly place, For ev-'ry na-tion, col-or, creed and race.

This lit-tle ba-by's gon-na change the world, in the

This lit-tle ba-by's gon-na change the world in the

CD: 22
D.S. al Coda
hearts of men, wo-men, boys and girls.
What did they
D.S. al Coda
hearts Oo
D.S. al Coda
Cadd 9/D
N.C.
CODA
CD: 23
f
What did they
CODA
Je - sus is His name.
CODA
Bm/D
D/E
F♯m
F♯m/E
DM7
F♯m7/E

46

Who would have tho't this ti - ny lad would hold all pow - er in His hand?

Oo

Tell me, what did they call Him?

King Je - sus is His

48

II. HIS MISSION – JESUS, THE SAVIOR
For Unto Us
with
When He Came

ISAIAH 9:6

G. F. HANDEL
Arr. by Joseph Linn

Arr. copyright © 1993 by Lillenas Publishing Co. All rights reserved.
Administered by Integrated Copyright Group, Inc., P.O. Box 24149, Nashville, TN 37202.

11
be up-on His shoul - der;
And the gov-ern-ment shall be up-on His shoul -
mf
11
Div.
And His name,
- der;
and His name shall be call-ed:
Won - der - ful
Div.
f
15
Coun - sel - or,
the Might-y God,
the Ev - er - last-ing Fa - ther, the
18

51

peace to the world when He came. To the many and the few and e-ven me and you, He bro't peace, last-ing peace when He came.

Sweet Little Jesus Boy

R. MacG.

ROBERT MacGIMSEY
Arr. by Joseph Linn

Freely, expressively ♩ = ca. 54

Sweet little Jesus Boy, they made You be born in a manger.

Sweet little Holy Child, we didn't know who You were.

Copyright © 1934 by Carl Fischer, Inc., New York. Copyright renewed.
International copyright secured. All rights reserved. Used by permission.

54

Didn't know You'd come to save us, Lord, to take our sins away. Our eyes were blind, we couldn't see, we didn't know who You were. Long time a-go, You were born, born in a man-ger low— sweet lit-tle Je-sus Boy. The

Oo Oo Oo Sweet lit-tle Je-sus Boy.

Oo

world treats You mean,___ Lord, treats me mean___ too; But that's how___ things are down here;___ we

57

don't know___ who You are. You have told us how; we are try-ing.___ Mas-ter, You___ have___ shown us how,

Oo___

Oo___

27
e- ven when You were dy - ing.
27
Unison
Just seems like we can't do right–
Unison
D/A
F♯m/A
A
D
D/F♯
27
A
Bm7
Aadd9/C♯
D
rall.
But please, Sir, for -
rall.
Look how we treat - ed You.
3
A
D
G
G/B
F♯m/A
rall.

give us, Lord, we did-n't know it was You.

Sweet lit-tle Je-sus Boy,

Sweet lit-tle Je-sus Boy,

born long time a - go,_____ Sweet____ lit - tle Ho - ly Child, we

born long time a - go,_____ Sweet____ lit - tle Ho - ly Child, we

(37) rit.
did - n't know who You were.

(37) rit. *Div.*
did - n't know who You were.

Praise to the Savior Medley

Arr. by Joseph Linn

Simply ♩ = 78

*"We Have Come to Worship Thee" (John W. Peterson)

We have come to worship Thee, Sav-ior of Is-ra-el. Grate-ful-ly

*Copyright © 1958, renewed 1986, arr. © 1993 by John W. Peterson Music.
All rights reserved. Used by permission.
Arr. © 1993 by Lillenas Publishing Co. All rights reserved.
Administered by Integrated Copyright Group, Inc., P.O. Box 24149, Nashville, TN 37202.

now do we bow at Thy feet.

We have come to worship Thee, Son of the Highest. Glad hearts we raise, Lord, Thy

*"Beautiful Savior" (German Hymn, tr. by Joseph Seiss – Tom Fettke, based on an Irish Folk Song)

*Copyright © 1973, 1993 by Pilot Point Music. All rights reserved.
Administered by Integrated Copyright Group, Inc., P.O. Box 24149, Nashville, TN 37202.

Sav - ior, King of Cre - a - tion, Son of God and Son of Man! Tru - ly I'd love Thee;

tru - ly I'd serve Thee, Light of my soul, my joy, my crown!

Beau - ti - ful Sav - ior, Lord of the

na - tions, Son of God and Son of Man! Glo - ry and hon - or, praise, ad - o - ra - tion,

Now and for-ev-er, for-ev-er more be Thine!

Quicker ♩ = 112
Unison "Praise the Lord! Ye Heavens, Adore Him" (From *Foundling Hospital Collection* – Franz Joseph Haydn)

Praise the Lord, for He is glo-rious; Nev-er shall His

67

promise fail. God hath made His saints victorious; Sin and death shall not prevail. Praise the God of our salvation! Hosts on high, His pow'r proclaim.

95
Heav'n and earth, and all cre - a - tion Laud and
D/F♯ DM7/F♯ GM9 G D/F♯ G GM9 A/C♯ D A F♯m/G A7/G
mag - ni - fy His
D/F♯ G A7 Bm
99
D/A A7sus A7
CD: 33
A little faster ♩ = 126
*"Blessed Be the Name of the Lord" (Clinton Utterback)
103
Add congregation (opt.)
name.
Bless - ed be the name of the Lord,
D B♭ A♭/B♭ B♭ C♭ D♭ E♭

Bless-ed be the name of the Lord,_____

Bless-ed be the name of the Lord,____ Most__ High._____

Bless-ed be the name of the Lord,_____ Bless-ed be the name of the Lord,

Bless-ed be the name of the Lord,_____ Most__ High.

The name of the Lord_____ is

a strong tow- -er, The righ-teous run in-

- to it and they are saved.

The name of the Lord is a strong tow-er, The righteous run in-to it

73

74

*Copyright © 1990 Integrity Hosanna! Music/ASCAP (c/o Integrity Music, Inc., P.O. Box 851622, Mobile, AL 36685-1622). All rights reserved. International copyright secured. Used by permission.

soul magnifies the Lord, and my spirit rejoices in God. For the Mighty One has done great deeds; I will follow Him as the Spirit leads. He has filled the hungry

160
with good things; Bless-ed be the Lord.
A7 A7/C♯ Dm
160
Gm7 C7sus C7 Dm
1 CD: 36
2
Bless-ed be the Lord. My Lord.
E♭M7 Gm/C B♭/C F F
165
poco rit.
Bless-ed be the Lord. Bless-ed be the Lord.
Gm7 C7sus C7 Dm E♭M7 C7sus F
poco rit.

Interlude II – The Reason for His Coming

JOSEPH LINN

Narr. 2 *(Interlude II music begins)* There could have been many reasons why God would have chosen to send His Son. Consider for a moment:

If our greatest need was for information, God would have sent an educator.

Narr. 1 If our greatest need was for technology, God would have sent an inventor.

Narr. 2 If our greatest need was for entertainment, God would have sent a performer.

Copyright © 1993 by Lillenas Publishing Co. All rights reserved.
Administered by Integrated Copyright Group, Inc., P.O. Box 24149, Nashville, TN 37202.

Narr. 1 If our greatest need was for money, God would have sent a banker.

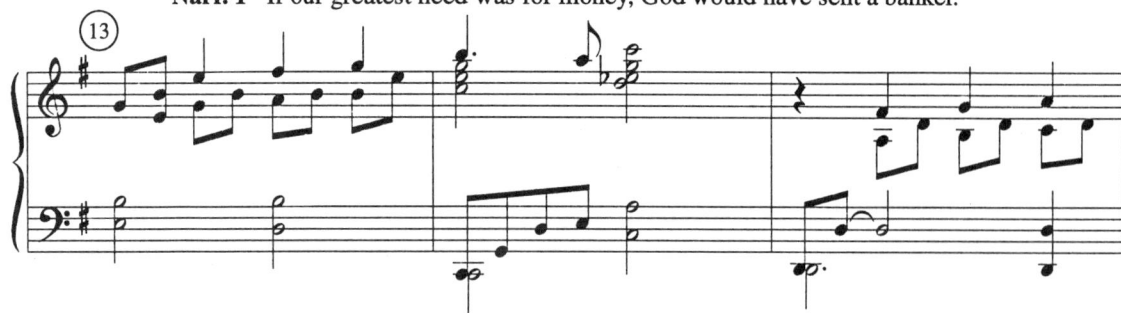

Narr. 2 But since our greatest need was for forgiveness, God sent . . . a Savior.

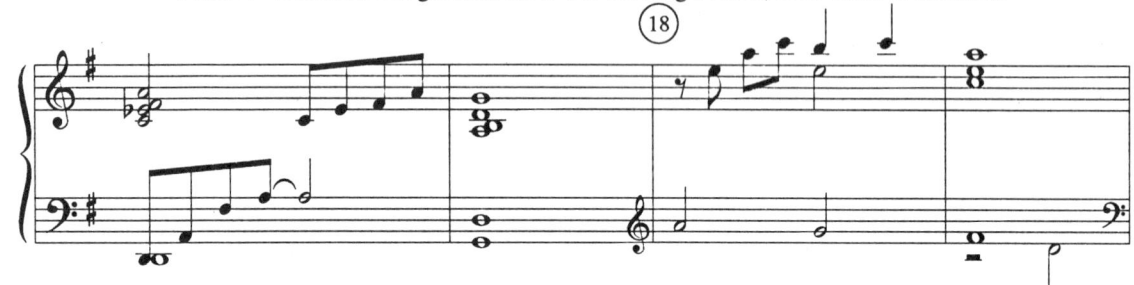

Narr. 1 "Who, being in very nature God, did not consider equality with God something to be grasped, but made himself nothing . . ."

Narr. 2 A Savior.
Narr. 1 "Taking the very nature of a servant, being made in human likeness . . ."

Narr. 2 A Savior.
Narr. 1 "Being found in appearance as a man, he humbled himself and became obedient to death– even death on a cross!" *(Phil. 2:6-9, NIV) (Music ends)*

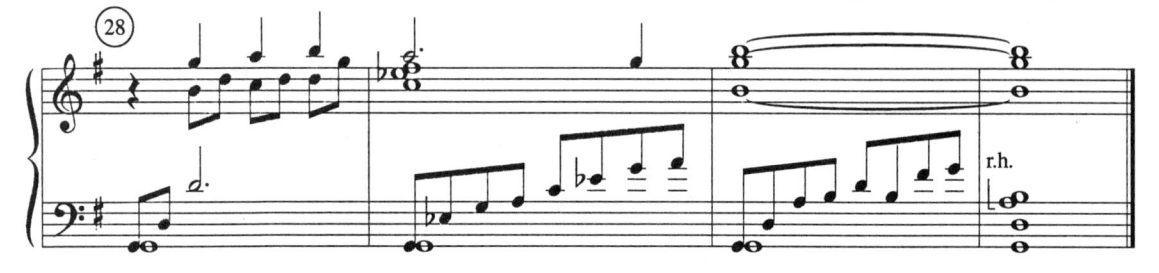

Love Was When

JOHN E. WALVOORD

DON WYRTZEN
Arr. by Joseph Linn

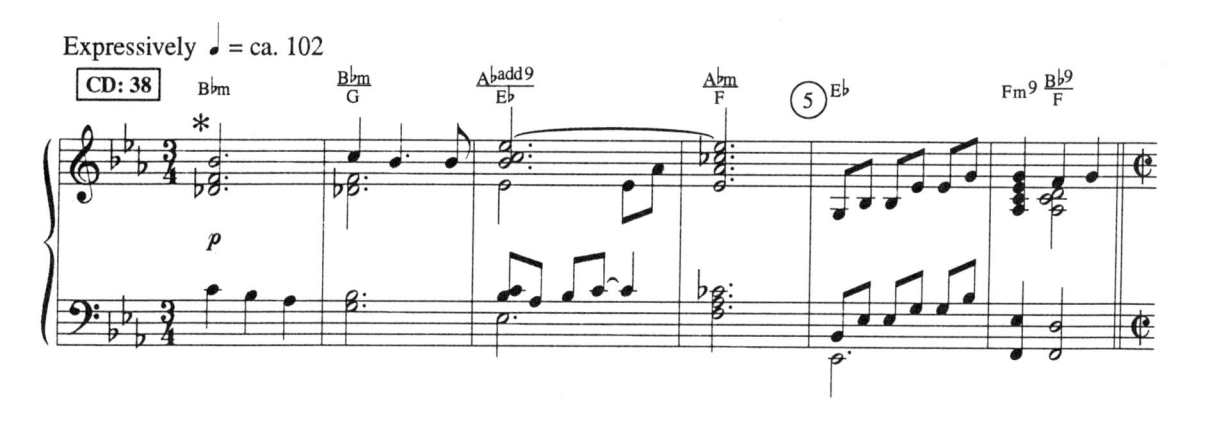

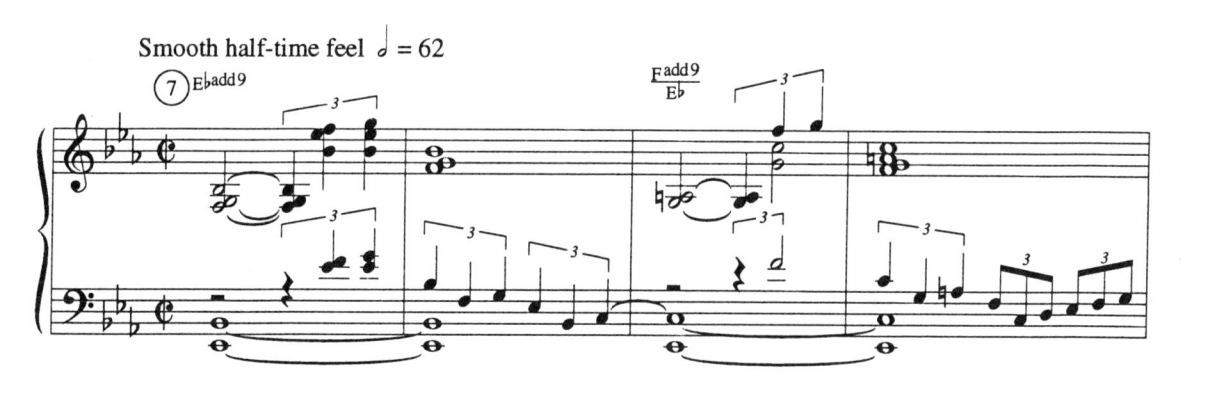

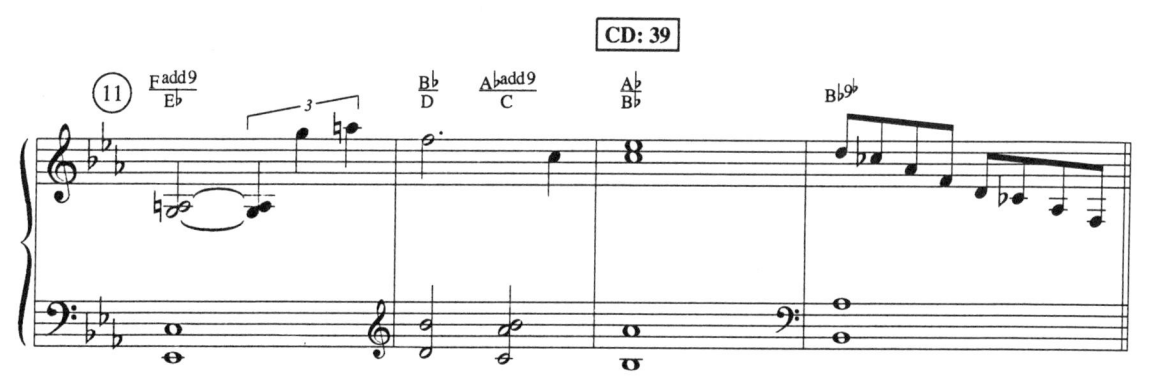

*First six measures and last eight measures from "God So Loved the World" (John Stainer)

Copyright © 1970 Singspiration Music (ASCAP). All rights reserved.
International copyright secured. Used by permission.

1. Love was when God became a man, Locked in time and space, without rank or place; Love was God born of Jewish kin, Just a

81

car - pen - ter with some fish - er - men.

Choir *mp*
Ah

Love was when Jesus walked in his - to - ry;

his - to - ry;

Lov-ing-ly He brought a new life that's free.

Lov-ing-ly He brought life, life that's free.

Love was God nailed to bleed and die To

Love was God, bleed and die

reach and love one such as I.

2. Love was when God be-came a man Down where

I could see love that reached to me.

Love was God dying for my sin, And so trapped was I, my whole world caved in. Ah

Love was when Jesus walked in his-to-ry;
his-to-ry;
Lov-ing-ly He brought a new life that's free.
Lov-ing-ly He brought life, life that's free.

71
a tempo
mf
Love was God nailed to bleed and die To
Unison
Love was God, bleed and die
Eadd9
F♯9/E
75
reach and love one such as I.
rit.
p
Div.
Ah
B/D♯
Aadd9/C♯
A/B
B9
B13
tacet

87

III. HIS COMING AGAIN – JESUS, LORD OF ALL
When He Came

M. L.

MOSIE LISTER
Arr. by Joseph Linn

CD: 43 In two ♩ = 72

He bro't love to the world when He came. He bro't love to the

Copyright © 1983, 1993 by Lillenas Publishing Co. All rights reserved.
Administered by Integrated Copyright Group, Inc., P.O. Box 24149, Nashville, TN 37202.

89

came. He bro't hope to the world when He came. He bro't hope to the world when He came. To the rich man, to the

32
poor man, the beg-gar and the king– He bro't hope, liv-ing
Div.
Bm A/C♯ D G Gm6/B♭ 32 D/A D/F♯ G
3
f rit.
mel.
hope when He came, when He came. He bro't
D/A A7 Bm Bm/A Bm/G♯ Gm/B♭ Gm6/B♭
36 a tempo
rit.
mel.
(8)
hope, liv - ing hope when He came.
36 D/A D/F♯ G D/A A7sus A7 D
a tempo
rit.

In Majesty He Will Come

D.T. and M.T.

DICK and MELODIE TUNNEY
Arr. by Joseph Linn

Majestically ♩ = ca. 82

Born of a mighty God, sent from His heavenly throne, Given to reign over

Copyright © 1988 BMG Songs, Inc. (ASCAP)/Pamela Kay Music [adm. by The Copyright Co., Nashville, TN (ASCAP)]/May Sun Music (adm. by Keeling & Company, Inc., Nashville, TN). All rights reserved. International copyright secured. Used by permission.

kings__ and priests, the sins of man to a-tone, The Mes-si-ah will re-turn, the hour__ un-known__ to man.__ A fan-fare of praise will in-hab-it__ the earth as cre-a - tion re-joic - es in Him! In majesty He will come with the sound of the trum-pet to claim the re-deemed. In

maj - es - ty___ He will come– Je- sus the Sav-ior, e - ter-nal King. Ev-'ry knee in heav-en__ and earth will__ bow to this__ most ho - ly__ One.___ In

maj - es - ty_____ He will come.
Clothed in His re - gal robe, crowned in His sov-'reign-ty.____ The scep-ter of righ-teous-ness

in His hand, our Lord for e - ter - ni - ty.

His king-dom will have no end for those who have known God's grace. The saints of all a - ges will gath - er as one to

CD: 48
cresc.
rall.
joy-ful - ly look on His face. In
cresc.
B♭
E♭/B♭
Fsus/B♭
F7/A
B♭sus
cresc.
rall.
55
a tempo
f
maj - es-ty He will come with the
f
55
Eadd9
Badd9/D♯
3
f a tempo
sound of the trum-pet to claim the re-deemed. In
Aadd9/C♯
Eadd9/B
Aadd9
B9sus
B9

59
stretch
a tempo
Div.
maj - es - ty He will come–
Div.
Fadd9
Cadd9/E
stretch
a tempo
63
Je - sus the Sav - ior, e - ter - nal King. Ev - 'ry knee in heav - en and
B♭add9/D
Fadd9/C
B♭
A
G/B
A/C♯
Dm
Dm7/C
Dm/B
earth will bow to this most ho - ly One. In
C
C/E
Fadd9
F/A
B♭
B♭/A
Gm7
Gm
Asus
A

maj - es - ty He will come.

In maj-es-ty, in maj-es-ty He will come.

Interlude III – An Invitation

JOSEPH LINN

(Interlude III music begins)
Narrator or Pastor *(conversational, with sincerity):* At the very center of Christmas is Jesus Christ.

He did not come merely to be a standard, a role model or an inspiration. He came to give us life.

The Bible says this story was written so "you may believe Jesus is the Christ, the Son of God, and that by believing you may have life in his name." *(John 20:31, NIV)*

Copyright © 1993 by Lillenas Publishing Co. All rights reserved.
Administered by Integrated Copyright Group, Inc., P.O. Box 24149, Nashville, TN 37202.

The Bible also paints a picture of Christ standing at the door of your heart, saying,

"Here I am! I stand at the door and knock. If anyone hears my voice and opens the door, I will come in." *(Rev. 3:20, NIV)*

Christ does not force Himself on anyone; you and I make that choice to let Him in.

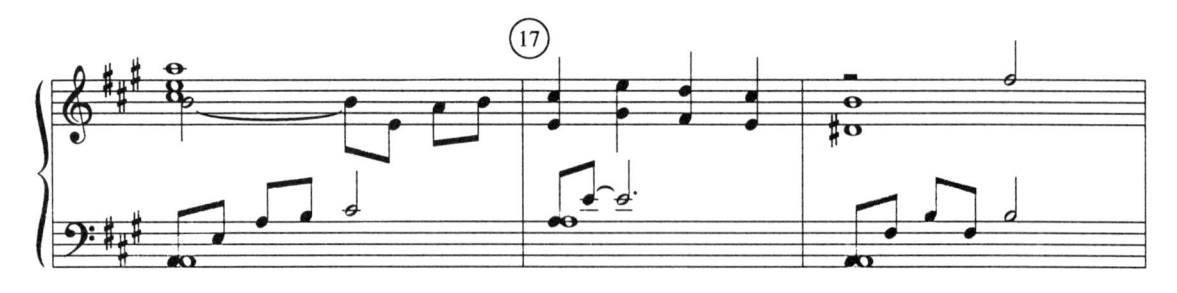

Since our greatest need is for forgiveness, God sent a Savior, and Jesus is His name.

Take Jesus With You

D. W.

DAN WHITTEMORE
Arr. by Joseph Linn

Copyright © 1993 by Lillenas Publishing Co. All rights reserved.
Administered by Integrated Copyright Group, Inc., P.O. Box 24149, Nashville, TN 37202.

sang_ of. Take Je - sus with___ you.___ He prom - ised us
A9/C♯ A/C♯ Bm7 A7/C♯ G/D D A Bm7 A7/C♯
14
free - dom.___ Re - ceive His sal - va - tion.___
Gm/D D A/G G Bm7/F♯
18
___ Now as we pray, trust Him to - day. Take Je - sus
Em7 G♯°7 D/A B♭9 Em A9

105

CHRISTMAS MUSICALS AS OUTREACH OPPORTUNITIES

Christmas is a great time of the year to attract nonattenders to your fellowship. The need for relationships, the holiday spirit, a general sense of things spiritual—all these help open doors of opportunity for inviting and ministering to others.

King Jesus Is His Name was written with this in mind. By using contemporary and traditional Christmas songs, the message of salvation in Jesus Christ is woven throughout. The themes are all in a Christmas context, covering Jesus' nativity as well as His life's mission and coming again. If your church is used to making a public invitation to accept Christ, an "invitation moment" is provided in the musical.

Lillenas Publishing Company and the writer pray you keep the nonbeliever in mind throughout. In order to help you, here are four key areas in planning for a successful outreach.

PRAYER—No amount of rehearsal or preparation can take the place of prayer. Colossians 3:16-17 urges that as we sing to one another, we do so in the name of Jesus. Consider these ideas in your prayer planning:

1. Challenge your choir with a prayer partner program, asking each to enlist someone not in choir during the weeks of rehearsal. This not only increases prayer but activates many others.

2. Pray for another church choir. The relationship will not only strengthen the impact of your ministry but make your choir members more aware of the larger ministry each church shares.

3. Create prayer reminders for your congregation. Tell them your ability to reach others is greatly enhanced by their prayer involvement.

PREPARATION—Once your prayer support is organized, plan your rehearsals.

1. Map out the weeks between your first rehearsal and the performance, detailing which songs will be rehearsed on which weeks; this way the entire work is evenly prepared. If you are singing from memory, provide your choir with memory target dates for each song. Communicate this when rehearsals begin so that your choir has the whole picture in mind. Use the Table of Contents in the front of this book as a ready reminder.

2. Secure the *King Jesus Is His Name* rehearsal tapes (MU-9153R) for individual rehearsal outside of choir.

3. Make soloist and narrator decisions early so that they have the time necessary to feel comfortable. Let narrators rehearse often with choir for ease of timing and flow.

PRODUCTION—*King Jesus Is His Name* is presented as a more concert-style musical; there are no characters or story line. The narrations provided are transitions to focus the meaning of the songs for the audience. Your church may desire more dramatic action, which is certainly an option.

In planning the production, keep these things in mind:

1. Plan for a strong visual effect. Christmas is highly visual with color and strong symbolism. Use it to create interest even before the music begins. Lighting, sets, decorations, and clothing all communicate.

2. Create a warm atmosphere from the very beginning. Impact the visitor with friendliness and acceptance from the time they enter. Greeters should be gracious and people-oriented. Preservice music, live or recorded, should be expectantly

joyful. Remember, those who attend are giving their time and doing YOU a favor! Make them feel special.

3. Involve technical support people (lights, sound, media, stage, etc.) from the beginning. Their contributions are vital, and their preparation is as important as any singer or orchestra member.

4. People movement to, from, and around the platform/choir area should be carefully scripted and rehearsed. The more people feel comfortable and prepared, the more relaxed and confident they will be in performance.

PROMOTION—Good public communication does not just happen; you need to know the community and its most effective publicity channels. Use the following simple time line as a basis for planning your publicity. You are only limited by your creativity.

8 WEEKS PRIOR:
- Determine your main target groups, both inside and outside of your church, making plans to reach each one.
- Determine your printing needs: tickets, fliers, posters, service folders (order MC-81SF service folders for this musical from Lillenas or your local dealer).

6 WEEKS PRIOR:
- Finalize artwork and needed information for printer.
- Confirm deadlines for news releases, radio spots, public service announcements; check photos to send with news releases or take photos if necessary.

5 WEEKS PRIOR:
- Submit artwork to printer.
- Organize distribution team: choir, orchestra, volunteers.
- Order or create large sign for outdoor publicity.

4 WEEKS PRIOR:
- Begin poster/flier distribution to congregation.
- Take fliers and posters to local business and community centers.

3 WEEKS PRIOR:
- Hang large sign outside.
- Begin ticket distribution (free or with donation).

2 WEEKS PRIOR:
- Pictures/news releases to local media as requested.
- Finalize printing of service folder, inserts.
- Increase publicity to church (phone calling, live announcements, etc.).

1 WEEK PRIOR:
- Final news releases to media as requested.

King Jesus
IS HIS NAME

King Jesus
IS HIS NAME

King Jesus
IS HIS NAME

King Jesus
IS HIS NAME

King Jesus
IS HIS NAME

King Jesus
IS HIS NAME

King Jesus
IS HIS NAME

King Jesus
IS HIS NAME

King Jesus
IS HIS NAME

King Jesus
IS HIS NAME